# VARICK'S NEWBURGH:
## HISTORY OF
## THE AFRICAN METHODIST EPISCOPAL ZION CHURCH
## OF
## NEWBURGH, NEW YORK
## 1827 – 2001

BY

## THE REVEREND DR. JANET DENISE JONES

**DORRANCE PUBLISHING CO., INC.**
PITTSBURGH, PENNSYLVANIA 15222

ISBN # 0-8059-5916-5
Printed in the United States of America

*First Printing*

For information or to order additional books, please write:
Dorrance Publishing Co., Inc.
643 Smithfield Street
Pittsburgh, Pennsylvania 15222
U.S.A.
1-800-788-7654
Or visit our web site and on-line catalog at *www.dorrancepublishing.com*

For
James and Aurelia
Joseph and Catherine
Frank and Vivian

# CONTENTS

# OPENING STATEMENT

## NEWBURGH, NEW YORK—A CASE STUDY

The title of this case study, *Varick's Newburgh: History of the African Methodist Episcopal Zion Church of Newburgh, New York 1827 to 2001*, was chosen for a specific reason. The title represents the last name of the church's denominational founder; Varick. Newburgh represents the city in which Varick was born. Thus *Varick's Newburgh* was chosen as the title for the case study of the local church in Newburgh from its birth in 1827 to 2001.

The research for this case study has taken place during years of active membership in the African Methodist Episcopal Zion Church of Newburgh, New York. Beyond personal experiences in the church, I have attempted to uphold a scholarly ethic in my approach to analyzing this delightful history. My methodology involved the use of primary and secondary sources, as well as the use of textual analysis. My historical analysis is based on interviews, texts, site visits, and observations. The photographs span several years of experience in the church, detailing artifacts, activities, and other important moments.

I believe the history of the African Methodist Episcopal Zion Church of Newburgh, New York is a remarkable account of endurance and survival. This church has weathered the miseries and triumphs of various eras: slavery and liberation; financial disasters and recoveries; health epidemics and healings; racial hatred and reconciliation. I believe the people of this local church have survived these difficulties and triumphs with a spirit of holiness, forgiveness, generosity, and strength.

Throughout this historical account, I believe you will meet people who were committed to keeping a church alive. The Lord was with this local congregation that is still thriving in this millennium. Other churches founded in Newburgh prior to or during the same period cannot speak of their survival and endurance: this is due to the fact that these churches did not survive.

However, I believe this local church has survived because of the strength and dedication of the leadership, membership, and most importantly, God's help.

After having the opportunity to write this historical account, I have become more and more aware of how the Lord blessed the African Methodist Episcopal Zion Church of Newburgh, New York with the gifts of perseverance, strength, and endurance. The Lord has kept the church alive to be of service to His Kingdom. That is why I believe this is a special church to God and humanity. This further proves this church's relevance to the changing contemporary issues of the day. A church that has had the fortitude to withstand the changing and diverse needs of people throughout generations must have the strength and guidance of the Holy Spirit. A church that has adapted its mission to meet the needs of two centuries of members without changing its thrust for evangelism is a holy place blessed by God.

The history of this local church is significant because it is connected to major movements in American history. It has been firmly established that leaders of the African Methodist Episcopal Zion Church of Newburgh, New York were leaders in the Underground Railroad, Abolitionist Movement, Civil Rights Movement, and other major acts working for economic, housing, and educational justice.

This analysis will cover how the church grew from 1827 to 2001. The African Methodist Episcopal Zion Church of Newburgh, New York is an example of a local congregation that has served humanity since the early 1800s. The local history of this church is a case study of a church that has survived years of triumph and tragedy. Overall, this is a profile of leadership and of a church's attempt to reach out to a community and promote spiritual wholeness.

The following are the theme, mission, goals, and conditions for membership set forth by the Reverend Frank Edward Jones, Pastor of the African Methodist Episcopal Zion Church of Newburgh, New York from 1964 to June 2001.

### The Theme of the Church
A Spirit-Filled Church Praising and Celebrating
the Resurrection of Jesus and the Power of the Holy Spirit

### The Mission of the Church
Proclaim to every people, tongue, and nation the God, in whom they live and move, is love: Tell how He stooped to save His lost creation, and died on earth that man might live above. Publish good tidings, tidings of peace, tidings of Jesus, redemption, and release.

## The Goals of the Church

To find, bring, and win unchurched and lost souls for participation in Christ's Kingdom.

To persuade persons to become disciples and responsible members of the Body of Christ, the Church.

To train church members for fulfilling this Commission of Christ

To edify Church members for Christian growth and maturity.

To create, develop, and maintain a deeper sense of love and caring among Church members.

To recultivate and reclaim delinquent members.

To expand the Outreach Ministry.

## Conditions for Membership

Believe in Jesus Christ as Lord and Savior.

Have an earnest desire to be saved from your sins.

Decide to follow Jesus and to serve Him, not based upon worthiness of ourselves, but solely on the merits of our Lord Jesus, His death, and intercession for us.

Hold sacred the ordinances of God, endeavor to promote the welfare of the Redeemer's Kingdom, and be governed by the Rules of the A.M.E. Zion Church.

Contribute to the support of the Gospel.

Endeavor to lead a holy life, following the commandments of God.

Reverend Jones is currently the Presiding Elder of the New York City District, and President of the Ministers' and Lay Association of the African Methodist Episcopal Zion Church.

Throughout the writing of this case study, I was given much support by my family and friends. I want to thank my parents, the Reverend Frank E.

Jones and Mrs. Vivian I. Love Jones for their continued support, love, and encouragement. This could not have been written without the trail blazers and torch bearers in the African Methodist Episcopal Zion Church of Newburgh, New York. I give special thanks to the members and allies of the church who rest with the triumphant majority in Heaven, and to those who continue to carry out the mission of the church. I respectfully acknowledge the Right Reverend George Washington Carver Walker, Sr. and Mrs. Geraldine Jackson Walker, Presiding Bishop and Missionary Supervisor of the North Eastern Episcopal District.

# CHAPTER ONE

JAMES VARICK,
THE FOUNDER AND FIRST BISHOP OF
THE AFRICAN METHODIST EPISCOPAL ZION CHURCH

The African Methodist Episcopal Zion Church exceeds beyond the North American continent reaching Africa, Great Britain, India, the Caribbean, and other prominent sites. This denomination first started as a church for Blacks, but has spread geographically and multiculturally throughout the world. Although the denomination has grown into a global church, Newburgh, New York is the site of its important beginning.

The founder and first bishop of the African Methodist Episcopal Zion Church was James Varick, and he was born on June 17, 1750. His birth was exactly 47 years after the founder of Methodism John Wesley in 1703. Varick and Wesley were born on the same day, June 17.

> It is stated by the early fathers of the church that he (James Varick) was born in Newburgh, N.Y., up the Hudson River from New York City. While Varick was born in Newburgh, it appears that his mother was a resident of New York and was on a visit when Varick was born (Wheeler, 1906, 9).

An African Methodist Episcopal Zion Church scholar, Bishop William J. Walls noted that Varick was:

> Born in Orange County, near Newburgh, N.Y., in 1750. His mother was a Negro slave of the household of Varicks of Dutch decent, who settled in Hackensack, N.J., as early as 1687. His father, Richard Varick, was born and baptized in the Dutch Church of Hackensack in 1720, and later moved to New York with his family. Members of the Varick family, with their slaves, were from time to time in the

Newburgh, Highland Falls, and the West Point area, as well as New York City, before and during the Revolutionary War (Walls, 1974, 84).

Varick spent his early years in New York City where he was raised, educated, and converted. It is speculated that Varick became a Christian as a young man during the famous preaching visitations of Philip Embury and Captain Thomas Webb in New York City. Embury and Webb were early Methodist evangelists who traveled and preached the Gospel from city to city. Most likely, Varick heard these evangelists, which served as the impetus for him to join the John Street Methodist Episcopal Church. "This church is the cradle of American Methodism and the place where Varick got his first religious training" (Wheeler, 1906, 11).

Methodism was an attractive denomination for Blacks because its founder, John Wesley, preached against slavery. Wesley established the Methodist church in England and it spread to the United States. In 1774, John Wesley wrote *Thoughts on Slavery*, which stated his strong opposition to slavery. Bishop William J. Walls also recorded Wesley's thoughts on slavery in his book, *The African Methodist Episcopal Zion Church: Reality of the Black Church*.

> You have seen them torn away—children from their parents, parents from their children; husbands from their wives, wives from their beloved husbands; brethren and sisters from each other. You have dragged them who had never done you any wrong, perhaps in chains, from their native shore. You have forced them into your ships like a herd of swine; them who had souls immortal as your own; only some of them leaped into the sea, and resolutely stayed under water, till they could suffer no more from you. You have stowed them together as close as ever they could lie, without any regard to decency or convenience. And when many of them have been poisoned by foul air, or had sunk under various hardships, you have seen their remains delivered to the deep, till the sea should give up his dead. You have carried the survivors into the vilest slavery, never to end but with life (Walls, 1974, 21).

Although John Wesley was vehemently opposed to slavery, not all Methodist parishioners in the United States acted upon the positions of the founder. The African Methodist Episcopal Zion Church was founded in 1796 because of the unjust treatment encountered in the John Street Methodist Episcopal Church in New York City. After enduring unjust and brutal treatment in this church, John Varick led a movement to begin a church with a thrust for and on behalf of Black people. He became a leader in the movement for equality and was able to accomplish several outstanding missions for the cause of humanity.

James Varick was an educator, theologian, suffragist, entrepreneur, writer, orator, and abolitionist. As a forerunner of the Abolitionist Movement, James Varick touched the following areas: emancipation, burial rights, education, voting rights, media access, religious freedom, and organizations for the support of Blacks. These were the seven privileges that were denied to Blacks that were attending the John Street Methodist Episcopal Church in New York City.

Varick, along with other African American members of this church, led a movement for equality and justice. Although the law prohibited Blacks from organizing, Varick defied the law that prohibited these activities. He assembled groups of friends at his house to strategize and combat the caste system in religion and government.

> One of the outstanding points in history of the Black race in this country is its poor, almost impossible, burial accommodations. New York Negroes confronted this condition as early as 1722, when the 'dread of an uprising of Blacks prompted an act providing that all Negroes and Indians should be buried by daylight. The act was amended afterwards that not more than twelve Negroes should attend a funeral. The penalty for the violation of this statue was public flogging. Furthermore, the slave was to be buried without any outward sign of grief or any ceremonial tokens, such as pall, gloves, or flowers.'…However, the denial of a decent burial for Black people existed when the African Methodist Episcopal Zion Church was born (Walls, 1974, 67).

Although these unjust and harsh rules were still enacted, the new members of the African Methodist Episcopal Zion Church fought against them following the establishment of the church. While members of the John Street Methodist Episcopal Church, the Blacks were not allowed to be buried on the church grounds at all. Furthermore, Blacks were not allowed to be buried in any church-owned burial grounds until James Varick and other community leaders fought to change this law in New York.

> The city did not allow Negroes to be buried in White or church-owned cemeteries, although they were members of various congregations, rather in an undesirable spot north of the Alms-house and Bridewell known as the Negroes' Burial Grounds. This brought Black men into political

> action in 1795 and they made petitions to the city gov-
> ernment for improvement of burial places and for the
> privilege of observing rights. ... After Zion (African
> Methodist Episcopal Zion Church) was built in 1800, its
> membership continued to swell. People of the Black race
> pined for a religious burial service with interment in a
> church burial ground. This being the only Black Church
> in the city of New York until the founding of the African
> (Abyssinian) Baptist Church in 1808, Zion Church's bur-
> ial ground by 1807 far exceeded the number for which it
> was built, as had the vault built under the church, with
> something like 750 bodies interred in the last five years
> (Walls, 1974, 67).

Religious burial rights were only one part of the religious caste system that needed to be abolished: religious freedom was a right that Blacks did not possess. They did not possess the right to preach freely or acquire an ordi- nation. Merely having the license to preach without the ordination to fully conduct all religious rights was an outrage. Hence, it became necessary to leave the church and establish an entry point for other Blacks interested in the ordained ministry.

> Varick was first privileged to exhort and then licensed to
> preach by the Quarterly Conference of the John Street
> Methodist Episcopal Church, and 'because of race friction,
> held separate religious meetings for his people as early as
> 1780.' ... In 1796 about 30 Negroes, under the leadership
> of James Varick, withdrew from the John Street Methodist
> Episcopal Church, and formed the first colored church of
> New York (Walls, 1974, 86).

Varick continued his fight for ordination, along with two other men of God, Thompson and Scott. They all had visions of what they wanted to accomplish for Christ through a successful ministry. Finally, Varick, Thompson, and Scott graduated to receive their deacon's orders in 1806. The three men became the first Blacks ordained in New York State.

The historical accomplishments of James Varick vary among areas of education, economics, politics, emancipation, enfranchisement, and reli- gious freedom. He was also active in starting the first Black newspaper in America, "The Freedom's Journal" in New York City. The newspaper oper- ated out of the African Methodist Episcopal Zion Church and continued to warn Blacks about the oppression they faced as a result of the law and the- ological interpretations.

Even though the African Methodist Episcopal Zion Church had been established for approximately fifty years, segregation was still practiced in many northern churches.

> They exposed the contradiction of the churches merciless-
> ly, and challenged the sincere believer to examine the doc-
> trine of true religion. For one year, May 4, 1827 to May 2,
> 1828, "The Freedom's Journal" operated from the com-
> modious and spacious facility of Zion Church at 152
> Church Street. An advertisement in "The Freedom's
> Journal" shows the interest of the leading Black preachers
> of the city in furthering the cause of education." B.F.
> Hughes operated a school at St. Philip's Episcopal Church,
> and James Varick was one of the supporters even thought
> there was also a school in Zion supported by its members
> (Walls, 1974, 92).

Varick, in addition to being a shoemaker, tobacco cutter, and pastor, ran a classroom at the church and in his own home. Later, the New York Manumission Society founded a school for Black children which was housed in Zion in the later 1700s. Varick also had a profound influence on the Abolitionist Movement. He was the first Black preacher in United States history to preach about abolition in 1807. Ironically, as Varick and other ministers were fighting for the abolition of slavery, they did not have the right to vote. This was another hurdle to cross, and again, Varick proved himself to be a leader in the early struggle for voting rights for Blacks.

Four major leaders in the movement for the advancement for Blacks have a direct relationship to James Varick and the African Methodist Episcopal Zion Church. They too were a part of Varick's thrust set in Zion's annals of History. Frederick Douglas, who was an orator, writer, abolitionist, preacher, and politician, was a member of the African Methodist Episcopal Zion Church. He received his license to preach in the Second Street African Methodist Episcopal Zion Church in New Bedford, Massachusetts. Throughout his life while working towards emancipation of the slaves, his spiritual fortification came from this denomination.

Harriet Tubman, Conductor of the Underground Railroad, was a member of the African Methodist Episcopal Zion Church in Auburn, New York, which is now named after her. Her Underground Railroad consisted of African Methodist Episcopal Zion Churches throughout the North. Forty years after her death in 1913, Ms. Tubman's house in Auburn, New York became the Harriet Tubman Home of the African Methodist Episcopal Zion Church. This historical monument was also part of Senator Hillary Rodham Clinton's "Save America's Treasurers Tour" during her tenure as First Lady.

Sojourner Truth joined the African Methodist Episcopal Zion Church in New York City around 1829. She was a spirit filled anti-slavery orator who later became an activist in the Woman's Suffrage Movement.

Booker T. Washington was the founder of Tuskegee Institute that originated in the Butler Chapel African Methodist Episcopal Zion Church in 1881. The school operated out of this church for two years and then expanded.

There are numerous members of this denomination who have influenced the history of the United States, not only African Americans. James Varick, the founder and first bishop of the denomination, is credited with having been the spiritual mentor to many leaders throughout the United States. It is understandable that this denomination and its members have such pride in the church, and also in Newburgh, New York where the founder was born.

James Varick was the cornerstone of movements that shaped, propelled, and improved the livelihood of African Americans in the United States. Varick served as the first bishop of the denomination following his consecration on July 30, 1822. Varick would have celebrated the fifth anniversary of his consecration in 1827, but died eight days prior. Bishop James Varick died on Sunday, July 22, 1827 in the morning. Varick was buried in the "colored section" of Woodlawn Cemetery in New Windsor, New York. Other prominent members of the African Methodist Episcopal Zion Church were buried in this section of Woodlawn Cemetery. It was the only burial ground available for people of color in the area. Therefore, there is a wealth of history located in this cemetery. In 1926 Varick's remains were removed from New Windsor, New York and placed in a crypt in the Mother African Methodist Episcopal Zion Church in New York City. The dedication of his crypt took place on February 1, 1926. The Varick family has had a profound influence on Christianity and the fight for social advancement of the African American people of the United States. The descendants of James Varick are often thought of as respectable people with a mind for social advancement and spiritual awareness.

The following five photographs are of the "colored section" of Woodlawn Cemetery, New Windsor, New York where Bishop James Varick was originally buried.

Photograph 1: The "colored entrance" to Woodlawn Cemetery in New Windsor, New York. The entrance is located next to the main road with easy access to the burial ground. This entrance was used to enter in and out of the "colored section" of the cemetery. It was used by those who participated in the original burial of Bishop James Varick, and other Zionites including Bishop and Mrs. Joseph P. Thompson.

Photographs 2-5: The area of the "colored section" of Woodlawn Cemetery in New Windsor, New York with the graves of the Thompsons,

Zionites who fought in the Civil War, local church members, and other influential African Americans from the area. The majority of the graves do not have any official records at the cemetery. Those who died prior to 1900 did not have any records kept on them; therefore it was the duty of the community to maintain the historical value of the area.

# CHAPTER TWO

## LOCAL HISTORY OF THE AFRICAN METHODIST EPISCOPAL ZION CHURCH OF NEWBURGH, NEW YORK

Continuing in the tradition of John Wesley, James Varick, and the movement for change is the African Methodist Episcopal Zion Church of Newburgh, New York. This local church is a special house of worship because it is located in the birthplace of the denomination's founder. It is known for its spiritual fire and community presence. The history of the African Methodist Episcopal Zion Church of Newburgh, New York dates back to 1827, making it the second Methodist Church and first African American Church in Newburgh. The history in Newburgh related to this denomination dates back even further, for Bishop James Varick, founder and first bishop of the denomination, was born in Newburgh in 1750. Following his death, he was laid to rest in the local area.

Not only can Newburgh be proud to be the birthplace of the founder, but it can also be proud of having several denominational leaders come out of the Newburgh Church. This local church has produced bishops, several general officers, Abolitionist leaders, Civil Rights leaders, and many other productive agents for change.

According to the early local church records, Rev. John Matthews headed the organization of the local church in May of 1827. The first meeting was held at the home of Caesar Sailor on Montgomery Street. Rev. Jacob Matthews, pastor of the African Methodist Episcopal Zion Church, New York, later took charge of the society, and sent his son, Rev. George Matthews, to preach.

In 1832, Rev. William H. Bishop assumed charge and services were held at Lewis Beattie's home on South Water Street. Later, the group moved to the basement of the Catholic Church on Liberty Street. In 1839, a lot on Washington Street was purchased from John W. Knevels, and a church building was erected under the pastorate of Rev. William H. Bishop.

From 1834 to 1847 the ministers in charge of the church were as follows:
The Reverend William Serrington
The Reverend Samuel Serrington
The Reverend Daniel Vanderveer
The Reverend George Garnet
The Reverend William H. Bishop
The Reverend John Tappan
The Reverend Richard Norris
The Reverend James Hall
The Reverend Henry A. Thompson
The Reverend John Dungy

Rev. Joseph P. Thompson who was born into slavery and became pastor in 1847 was a doctor as well as a preacher; he made a name for himself not only in Newburgh, but also throughout the world. He was later consecrated a bishop and was invited to England where he read a paper before the Ecumenical Conference of Methodist Churches. He died in Newburgh in 1894 and was buried in Woodlawn Cemetery. During his pastorate the Reverend R.E. Eastep assisted him, and plans were made for the incorporation of the church. These were completed in 1848.

In 1850, Rev. Samuel Giles became pastor, remaining for only one year. The Reverend Peter Ross, during whose pastorate the church was rebuilt, succeeded him. In 1856 the Reverend James Livingstone, who had been pastor for only a few months, died to be succeeded by Rev. I. C. Spencer.

Rev. Joseph P. Thompson, former pastor of the African Methodist Episcopal Zion Church of Newburgh, New York was called back in 1858 to serve for another four years. He paid off the church's debt and finished the vestry. *The History of the Town of Newburgh*, written in 1859, mentioned the church in its historical account of Newburgh.

> In addition to those already enumerated there are three churches composed of colored men. The first of these—the "African Methodist Episcopal Zion Church" has a neat edifice on Washington Street (Ruttenber 1859, 242).

This account was written during the pastorate of Rev. Joseph P. Thompson. Thompson is also noted for serving as the trustee of "The Colored School" on Washington Street in Newburgh.

> When the new Glebe School was opened in 1849, a school for African-American students opened on Washington Street in the vicinity of Washington's Headquarters. It was known as the 'colored school.' This school became part of

the Newburgh City School District in 1852, but it remained a segregated school for some time.

> Very little is known about this school. According to one of the oldest Newburgh Board of Education yearly reports, the school was still open in 1867. At that time, one principal and six teachers worked in the school. Unfortunately, neither their names nor the names of their children have been found (Favata, 1997, 75-76).

Twice the church had been attacked during Watch Meeting Services, the first being on December 31, 1860 when Joseph P. Thompson was the pastor. The second time was on December 31, 1862 when Rev. Jacob Trusty was the pastor. A number of rioters attacked the church each time. The first time they were arrested and fined one hundred dollars. The second time, they were broken up by a band of soldiers. These were racially motivated attacks, but the church was able to survive physical attacks against themselves and their property.

In 1863, Rev. William H. Decker was appointed pastor. During this year, Dubois Alsdorf assisted him in having the church repainted. New blinds were added; stoves bought; the church insured; and debt paid off. It was also important to clean up the damage done to the church on December 31, 1862. The church worked hard to keep the church going and in good condition.

In 1867, Rev. Joseph P. Thompson came back to be the pastor for the third time, and was later consecrated to the Bishopric. While pastoring, he accomplished the major task of buying the church organ; Professor Alsdorf was the organist. The Church School and other organizations used the organ after the new church was built. Mrs. Catherine Gillchrist Thompson, wife of the pastor, was the first Treasure of the Ladies' Home and Foreign Missionary Society. Rev. Mrs. N.H. Turpin was also elected an officer to the position of Corresponding Secretary.

Bishop Joseph P. Thompson and family, still residents of Newburgh, New York, were also known for their work on the Underground Railroad. The daughter of Bishop Thompson and his wife Catherine, married into the Alsdorf family. It was the Thompson's daughter, Mary, and her husband, Dubois Alsdorf, who ran the stop for the Underground Railroad in Newburgh. It is known that their inspiration for this work came from Catherine Gillchrist Thompson and her father, Simon C. Gillchrist.

> Mrs. Thompson inherited her zeal for freedom from her father, who was a noted Underground Railroad operator in Pennsylvania. During the dark years of slavery, she not only worked tirelessly to relieve the suffering of the slaves, but

she also devised clever schemes to help them escape to free territory (Johnson and Williams 1996, 21).

In addition to the research by Johnson and Williams, Bishop William J. Walls wrote another account of the family efforts in bringing slaves to freedom.

Roger King, author of *The Silent Rebellion: The Underground Railroad in Orange County, New York* discussed the significance of the Alsdorf family in Newburgh. King established that the Alsdorf household was the Newburgh stop on the Underground Railroad.

> The Newburgh Station of the Underground Railroad was the home of the Alsdorfs, prominent Negro Citizens of the village. The Alsdorfs had broken through the color line in a most unusual way. As professional dancing masters, they taught several generations of the White youth of Orange County their way through the mazes of the waltz or polka, or whatever dance of the day might be. But in the 1850s, they were carrying on an interesting sideline, in which very careful stepping played a part (King 1999, 17).

On page 58 of the Roger King book, the table entitled "Known Stations of the Underground Railroad" marks the Newburgh Station as "The Alsdorfs." Other indications also point to the significance of the Alsdorf Stop in Newburgh, New York. "Sometimes they (the Bull family) would send them (the fugitives) to Newburgh, with a note to the Alsdorfs, a well known and respected family of colored people, and when that was impractical they would send them up to Goshen" (King 1999, 26). The Alsdorfs carried on the tradition of the African Methodist Episcopal Zion Church also known as the Freedom Church by working for freedom as a stop on the Underground Railroad.

Additional scholars have remarked on how the entire family had a sense of commitment to social justice and religious fervor. Bishop and Mrs. Thompson have also been upheld for their team ministry; their commitment to discipleship and evangelism; their rhetorical and organizational skills; the development of denominational organizations; and their leadership in the Abolitionist Movement.

Mrs. Catherine Gillchrist Thompson is especially noted for her work in the Ladies' Home and Foreign Missionary Society as its first Treasurer. She founded the Sons and Daughters of Conference in Newburgh, New York. There is also a stained glass window in honor of this organization in the African Methodist Episcopal Zion Church, Newburgh, NY. She was praised for being a devout woman who studied the Bible with all seriousness. She applied her life to the Gospel and worked tirelessly for Jesus.

In Church service Mrs. Thompson excelled her peers; for no sacrificial task seemed to great for her to make as she labored in Christ's Kingdom. Her service was based on and directed by the Word of God; for the Bible was her book of books and her knowledge of it was remarkable. Indeed, her understanding and knowledge of the bible was comparable to the well-prepared clergy of her day. She was an invaluable helpmate to her clergy husband, who was also a medical doctor, missionary to Nova Scotia, and ecumenical leader. Bishop and Mrs. Thompson especially enjoyed spending long hours together discussing complicated scriptural doctrines (Johnson and Williams 1996, 21).

Although Bishop Thompson was no longer pastoring the African Methodist Episcopal Zion Church of Newburgh, his service continued in a new capacity. He and his wife continued to lead the denomination to greatness from their home in Newburgh, New York.

The African Methodist Episcopal Zion Church of Newburgh, New York was rebuilt in 1879 by Rev. Jacob Thomas, and it was rededicated by Bishop J.J. Clinton, assisted by Joseph P. Thompson, a three-time pastor of the church.

Succeeding pastors were Rev. Gabriel Rice, Rev. Henry Dumpson, and Rev. Nathaniel Stubbs. During the Stubbs pastorate, the bond and mortgage of the church were paid through a campaign led by Valentine Robinson and Charles B. Alsdorf.

In 1876, Rev. William Decker was named pastor for the second time. In succeeding years, the pastorate was filed by Rev. William H. Decker, Rev. Jacob Thomas, Rev. M.A. Rose or Ross, Rev. W.H. Turpin, Rev. J.A. Evans, Rev. J.B. Small, and Rev. John V. Givens.

In 1883, the church was painted when Rev. John Jones was pastor. Following him were Rev. T.W. Johnson, Rev. Alfred Day, and Rev. R.H., Stitt, the latter of who was leading the church when a new roof was put on the edifice. It was also under his leadership that the debt of the church was cancelled. The occasion was celebrated on March 16, 1890.

Many other pastors in succeeding years also led the church. These included Rev. E.G. Clitton or Clifton, Rev. P.H. Williams, Rev. S.J. Strother, Rev. D.C. Covington, Rev. W.J. Holland, and Rev. A.M. Walker.

The Reverend Lewis Day Williams assumed the pastorate in May of 1902. Two years later gas lights were installed, and one year after that, definite plans were made for a new church. The last service in the old church was held on Sunday, August 20, 1905, and the following day, demolition of the church began by the purchaser, William Peacy.

Through work and cooperation of both Black and White citizens, enough money was subscribed to complete the new church at a cost of

$10,876. Mrs. Elizabeth Merritt of Middle Hope, New York gave the pastor $3,000 to obtain the lot east of the church to be used for a parsonage. A brief biographical sketch was written about Mrs. Merritt in *The Portrait and Biographical Record: Orange County* and reads as follows:

> Miss Elizabeth M. Clark Merritt December 27, 1865: Mr. Merritt (Andrew H.) married Miss Elizabeth M. Clark, a native of New York City, where her parents, Thomas R. and Amelia (Smith) Clark, were also born. She was one of a large family, and lost her parents and a number of her brothers and sisters during the cholera epidemic of 1849. The only child of Mr. and Mrs. Merritt, Charles E., was born on January 8, 1868 and married, May 8, 1889, Miss America Earl, daughter of Peter and Hannah (Conklin) Earl, deceased. Four children were born to them, of whom, three daughters are living, Ethel, Laura, and Ada. In religious belief, Mrs. Merritt is connected with the Methodist Episcopal Church, to which our subject is a liberal contributor (Burrows 1994, 796-797).

Ground was broken for the new home, but the pastor did not live but a few days after this. He was succeeded by Rev. L.G. Mason, who upon being made Presiding Elder of the Hudson River District, and was followed by Rev. M.L. Harvey who served for three years. The next pastor was Rev. J.F. Waters; he cleared both the church and parsonage debts in 1914.

Succeeding pastors included Rev. L.H. Taylor, a Newburgher; Rev. Harry J. Williams, who instituted the first troop of Boy Scouts in the city; Rev. John T. Matthews; and Rev. Chanceford Fairfax. During the pastorate of the latter, the centennial of the church was celebrated for a period of three weeks from May 8-29, 1927. The historical program still exists in the archives of the church.

From 1928 to 1931, the pastor was Rev. H.E.W. Blount, followed by Rev. J.E. Walters, and Rev. E.O. Clarke who came in 1933 and remained until 1943. In 1943, the present pastor, Rev. Thomas McDougal was appointed by Bishop William J. Walls to take charge of the local church. While pastoring in Newburgh, expensive repairs were made to the church and parsonage, and the debt was cleared. The dual celebration marking the 150th anniversary of the African Methodist Episcopal Zion Church in America, and the founding of a local congregation 117 years ago was held in November of 1945 for one week. For the first time in the history of the denomination, the local church and community entertained the Connectional Conference and the Board of Bishops from July 28-August 1, 1948.

The next pastor was Rev. Charles Guita McKinney. He and his wife served the congregation for many years. Much of his pastorate is recorded in local church documents. Dr. McKinney is a published author and poet. He was later appointed to serve as the Presiding Elder of the Hudson River District, and served until 2000. His wife, the late Mrs. Bessie McKinney served as the President of the Hudson River District WH&OM Society. They have one daughter, Dara.

Following Dr. McKinney, Rev. Lee Clinton Siler served the church from 1952 to 1960. Under his leadership, the church and parsonage received upward of fifteen thousand dollars worth of repairs. Rev. Siler's service in the church is still remembered and is documented in the local church records. The Reverend Aaron T. Hoggard was the next pastor of the church. He recently passed away in February of 2001. Following Rev. Hoggard was the interim pastor Rev. T.H. Brooks; his term lasted approximately six months.

The early history of the church proudly recognizes lay activity upon which the current membership was able to build. Mention should be made of some of the very good friends and supporters of the African Methodist Episcopal Zion Church of Newburgh, New York. Mrs. Anna Bourne was interested in the welfare of the church when she first attended a service there and her father filled the pulpit. Upon her death, she bequeathed money to the local church. Members of the African Methodist Episcopal Zion Church of Newburgh also have expressed thanks to attorneys such as Peter Cantline who have aided the church. Miss Elizabeth Merritt of Middle Hope was especially generous when funds were collected for the new church, and then upon her death she bequeathed five thousand dollars to the church in trust. Mrs. Goldsmith Johnes left the church two thousand dollars. A donation by Thomas Thayer made possible the purchase of a pipe organ, and J. Elwood Easman assisted to make possible the installation of the musical instrument. Another supportive and financial friend was Mrs. Delano Hitch.

## Contemporary History of the African Methodist Episcopal Zion Church
## of
## Newburgh, New York

In 1964, the Reverend Frank Edward Jones came to the local church to serve as the pastor. He was the pastor of this church until June of 2001, and has served this local congregation longer than any other pastor in its history. He has also made denominational history with the extended length of a single pastoral charge. In all his years of pastoring, Rev. Jones never took a sabbatical from the pulpit. He was consistent in his pastoral leadership for the entire duration of his charge. Presently, he serves as the Presiding Elder of the New York City District.

The wife of Rev. Jones, Mrs. Vivian I. Love Jones, has been an active, creative, and successful partner in ministry. While working as a teacher, she vigorously served the local church with her husband as a Licensed Exhorter. Reverend and Mrs. Jones are both renowned speakers domestically and internationally. Additionally, Rev. Jones has been on several radio and television broadcasts speaking on issues of housing and economic justice. He has been in several magazines and newspapers in the local community and nationally.

Rev. Jones, in a native of Mobile, Alabama where he was an active member of State Street African Methodist Episcopal Zion Church. He is the son of Louis and Francis Jones. His mentors were his Pastor and First Lady of State Street African Methodist Episcopal Zion Church, the Reverend Charles Cecil Coleman and Mrs. Alcestis McCollough Coleman. At the age of 16, Rev. Jones preached his trial sermon at the State Street African Methodist Episcopal Zion Church under Rev. Coleman. His trial sermon, "No One Can Serve Both God and Mammon," was well received.

Rev. Coleman continued to mentor Rev. Jones even after he was elevated to the bishopric. Bishop Coleman, along with Bishop Herbert Bell Shaw, were significant forces in the life of the former pastor. The late Bishop William Milton Smith also had a special relationship with Rev. Jones and his family in Mobile, Alabama. Additionally, his advisor and academic mentor, Dr. John Henry Satterwhite, taught him and spent significant time with him. Other special mentors throughout his life influenced him intellectually, spiritually, and creatively.

Rev. Jones was educated at Livingstone College and Hood Theological Seminary in Salisbury, North Carolina. Rev. Jones was the valedictorian of his graduating class at Hood Theological Seminary. He continued his education by studying at Harvard Divinity School where he studied under the famous theologian, Professor Paul Tillich. While living in Massachusetts, Rev. Jones continued to work for the National Shawmut Bank of Boston. Rev. Jones currently continues to maintain several academic and business interests.

Mrs. Jones is a graduate of Talladega College in Talladega, Alabama where she was an English major. Later, Mrs. Jones completed a Master of Arts Degree in the Teaching of English at Columbia University's Teachers College in New York City. Beyond this degree, she completed further study in Applied Linguistics. Mrs. Jones is certified to teach on all levels in New York State. She also served as the Head Teacher of English at South Junior High School in Newburgh.

Under the leadership of Rev. and Mrs. Jones in 1971, one of the church's major projects was the sponsoring, construction, and completion of Varick Homes at the cost of 2.5 million dollars. Rev. Jones was responsible for the initiation, construction, and managing of Varick Homes, a one hundred twenty-two unit multi-family housing complex. This project was a government-insured development and is located on the Hudson River in the City of Newburgh. Both Rev. and Mrs. Jones shared a significant role in accomplishing this project for the good of humanity.

The late Bishop William J. Walls, author of *The African Methodist Episcopal Zion Church: Reality of the Black Church* (1974), wrote about this significant accomplishment in his book on page 549: "Among the housing projects completed or near completion by 1972 were the Varick Apartments, led by the Washington Street African Methodist Episcopal Zion Church in Newburgh, N.Y., Rev. Frank E. Jones, pastor." This project has also been documented in several papers, television reports, and books in the nation. It received further documentation in *Newburgh, NY: Portrait of a River City* by Ricardo Hinkle in 1998. A host of aerial and ground photos document Varick Homes and its significance in the local area.

Rev. Jones has had over 25 years of experience in developing, constructing, and managing multi-family housing. In Mount Vernon, New York, he was the consultant of Greater Centennial Homes, a 156 multi-family complex at the cost of 5.6 million dollars. This project was a government-insured development. Additionally, he was the consultant for the development and construction of Burton Towers, a senior citizens' housing complex of 126 units at a construction of 3.8 million dollars. This project is located in the city of Newburgh.

Continuing his commitment to helping those in need, Rev. Jones was also the Executive Director of Newburgh Community Action Committee, Inc. located at 257 Liberty Street. Rev. Jones was the founder of Newburgh Community Action Committee, Inc. and it has spread out to other locations in the Newburgh Area. Newburgh Community Action Committee, Inc. is an important community action agency in New York State and around the United States. Newburgh Community Action Committee, Inc. has also won numerous recognitions and citations for its outstanding work servicing people in need and for its implementation of programs. The Newburgh Community Action Committee, Inc. is a multi-million dollar establishment that is committed to community outreach and improvement.

During the pastoral leadership of Rev. Jones, many accomplishments were made. He served two successful terms as the International President of the Ministers and Lay Association from 1985 to 1993. He was recently elected to serve another term as the President of the Ministers and Lay Association in March of 2001. He changed the name of the organization from the Ministers and Laymen's Association to the Ministers and Lay Association to include gender equality in the organizational name. He is also known for taking on a significant fight for ministerial justice during his presidency. The resolution and its significant victory are noted in the 1988 General Conference Minutes where Rev. Jones addressed the international delegation in Charlotte, North Carolina. Rev. Jones continues his activities with this organization, and provides leadership in other capacities. His expertise is sought out by many in the denomination.

Rev. Jones has also held membership on the following boards: Ranking Member—The Codification Committee; Member—The Hood Theological Seminary Administrative Board; and Member—The Brotherhood Pension Committee. Rev. Jones also works closely with activist around the nation for issues of justice.

Rev. Jones has served numerous times as a delegate to the General Conference and recently served as a delegate to the 2000 General Conference in Greensboro, North Carolina. He was first elected a delegate in 1972 and has served as a delegate to every General Conference since then. In 1988, he served as the Leader of the New York Conference Delegation to the General Conference. At the 1996 and 2000 General Conferences, he held the position of Chairman of the Revision Committee. He is also the author of the Constitution for the African Methodist Episcopal Zion Church. The Constitution was adopted at the 1996 General Conference in Washington, D.C.

Mrs. Vivian I. Love Jones has also served the denomination by serving as a delegate to the General Conference in 1984, 1988, 1992, 1996, and 2000. Her participation in the General Conference included serving as Chairperson of the Harriet Tubman Home, Secretary of the Executive and Judiciary Committee, and member of various other General Conference Committees.

The ecumenical involvement of Mrs. Jones includes work with The National Council of Negro Women, Church Women United, and the World Federation of Methodist and Uniting Church Women. She has served as an African Methodist Episcopal Zion representative to the affiliate meetings of the National Council of Negro Women. Her involvement with Church Women United consisted of reactivating the then defunct unit of Newburgh, New York, where she served as the president and initiated some exciting projects. She is the past New York State Vice President for Ecumenical Action and the Mid-Hudson Area Chairperson for Church Women United.

Her leadership with the World Federation of Methodist and Uniting Church women included representing the African Methodist Episcopal Zion Church as a workshop leader on family life at the North America Area Meeting in Antigua. She has been the one to organize the World Federation Day Observances in the local area.

Rev. and Mrs. Jones continued to serve the entire denomination while also attending to the needs and interests of the local church. In their ministry together, they have made domestic and international travel a priority; they have seen several continents around the world. They also traveled extensively for the purpose of growing as a couple and obtaining new information for the church. This was a significant part of their lives so that they could grow and share new information with the local congregation. Together, they also take a special ministry retreat each year to make plans for the conference year. This is their time to meditate, seek God's will and plan. They have also challenged themselves throughout the years to remain committed to the work of missions in the Caribbean.

Mrs. Jones began her "Lunches With the Pastor's Wife" several years ago, and these lunches grew into women's retreats for the local church. The women of the African Methodist Episcopal Zion Church of Newburgh have enjoyed Spirit-filled weekend retreats at various locations around the state of New York. Special women preachers have been included to minister to the needs of each woman.

Mrs. Jones travels around the world to historical sites, religious meetings, and other conferences. In 1999, she successfully implemented the first trip to the Holy Land and Egypt for the women of the local church and the greater Newburgh community. The Reverend Frank E. Jones led a Sunday service entitled "The Pastoral Blessing of the Women's Delegation to the Holy Land and Egypt."

Each woman who attended had the opportunity to speak and pray at different sites. The women had Holy Communion at the Garden Tomb of Jesus; took a boat ride on the Sea of Galilee; gather in Bethlehem, Tel Aviv, Tiberias, and Jerusalem; walked in the Jordan River, the Dead Sea, and along the Road to Jericho; drove across the Sinai Peninsula and the Suez Canal; visited the Pyramids in Cairo; and also spent a brief time in London visiting Buckingham Palace, Parliament, Victoria Station, and the Thames River. Additionally, during the summer of 1999, Mrs. Jones had the wonderful opportunity to address and bring greeting to two African Methodist Episcopal Zion Church congregations in London, England. She spoke at Ransom Pentecostal African Methodist Episcopal Zion Church and Trinity African Methodist Episcopal Zion Church. In January of 2000, Mrs. Jones was in Lucerne, Switzerland and in January of 2001, she was in Vienna, Austria to fulfill professional obligations.

Mrs. Jones also developed the Helen A. Coppedge Missionary Society of the African Methodist Episcopal Zion Church of Newburgh and served as the president for over 25 years. During her presidency, she was responsible for the visit of the African Delegation of Woman's Home and Overseas Missionary Society to Newburgh, New York. Mrs. Jones sponsored many retreats, raised money for missions, developed workshops, and implemented outreach endeavors. She held regular programs and monthly meetings for the society. Her activity on the local, district, and national levels is known throughout the denomination. Mrs. Jones revived the Home Missions Society of the local church and served as the president.

On January 1, 2000, the Millennium Plaque was presented to the church as a gift from Rev. and Mrs. Jones. It was for the purpose of recognizing the past laborers of the local church in Newburgh. May it serve as recognition of God's people working hard for their Lord and Savior Jesus Christ. A section of the plaque reads as follows:

> This plaque is dedicated to the pastors of this local church for their leadership, dedication, and commitment to God's people. As pastors of this local church, these men have preached the Gospel of Jesus Christ and completed great works for the advancement and preservation of God's people. As the church embarks on a new millennium, this plaque is a proud recognition of their pastoral leadership and labor during the past two centuries. May God's blessings be with each one who is called to Zion to further God's Will, to render service to His people, and to walk in His Divine Providence (The Millennium Plaque 2000).

Rev. and Mrs. Jones have also initiated historical archives of the local church in the Newburgh Free Library, where preservationists care for the precious documents

In the local church, many improvements have taken place with an active and vibrant membership. The church has been repainted, stenciled, and repaired on the inside and outside several times. The parsonage has also been painted and restored. The pulpit, chairs, pews, and other artifacts were refurbished.

The air conditioners have been replaced two times; new carpet was replaced on both levels of the church; the pews and doors were beautifully refurbished to their natural hue; new plaques and an outside monument have been added; a Hammond organ was added to the sanctuary; the stained glass windows received extensive maintenance treatments; the bathrooms updated; and a water cooler and boiler installed. The parking lot across the street from the church was paved and other buildings were built during the pastorate of Rev. Jones. The local church is also remembered for its lovely decorations, architecture, and interior design features.

Spiritually, the local church saw growth. Rev. and Mrs. Jones implemented the Monday Night Bible Class. This class was taught by Rev. and Mrs. Jones for many years. Mrs. Jones started the Friday Morning Prayer, which met during sunrise. The church grew to become a tithing church where the members take utmost pride in giving their tithes to the Lord. The church annually celebrated Lent with special Wednesday night services and fasts during the entire season. Each year, the church had a lovely sunrise service with a breakfast sponsored by the Men's Club. The church celebrated Advent with special candles and Pentecost by wearing of red. The church recognized the seasons of the church year with the colors of the pulpit, bulletins, and the pastor's stole matching each season. The church continually has regular Quarterly Conferences and successfully fulfills the mandates placed on the church.

Throughout the tenure of Rev. Jones, several men and women have ministered to the local congregation under his leadership. The church recognizes the late Reverend Petty D.W. McKinney who assisted Rev. Jones for several years. The late Reverend Evangeline Phason Bell was a part of the ministry of this church until her death. The late Reverend Arthur Jones was also a significant help to Rev. Jones and was a dedicated servant to the church. Other ministers of significance to the ministry include Rev. Charles Lewis, Rev. Jesse Merritt, Rev. Ralph McGhee, Rev. Robert Holmes, Rev. Randolph Freeman, and Rev. Dr. Denise Jones.

Under the Jones' pastorate, the organizations in the church were alive, active, and well. Throughout the life of the Sunday School, both adults and children were spiritually filled with classes, activities, and trips. One historic visit to the Nation's Capitol in Washington, D.C. included memorable sightseeing and a visit to Congress. The Christian Education Department sponsored trips to theme parks, historical sites in New York State, and annual church meetings.

Under the leadership of Rev. and Mrs. Jones, the church had a new program on Saturday mornings offering church school, plus breakfast and lunch for young people. It was a thriving ministry in Christian Education. The local church also had a basketball ministry with a team call the Zion Lions, and also sponsored the Summer Sizzler, a youth basketball program. The former pastor also implemented the basketball ministry program.

Recent histories of the Newburgh community have included: the African Methodist Episcopal Zion Church, its members, or locations significant to its history in Newburgh. In 1997, C-SPAN came to Newburgh to follow the travels of Alexis de Tocqueville recorded in his book, *Democracy in America*. During the historical overview of this journey, C-SPAN recorded the historic Montgomery Street where the church had its start in May of 1827.

In 1998, Senator Hillary Rodham Clinton visited Newburgh on her "Save America's Treasures Tour." The Reverend Frank E. Jones was a special guest at her program, which was held only one block away from the church at George Washington's Headquarters. Rev. Jones has been a guest at the White House and received many high level elected officials at the church.

Recent scholarship within the denomination has continued to serve as a constant source of support both spiritually and intellectually. *The Varick Family* by Dr. B.F. Wheeler has been made available to the denomination thanks to Bishop J. Clinton Hoggard who in 1990 commissioned the reprinting of the original text. This book was written in the early 1900s about the life of James Varick. *Pioneering Women of the African Methodist Episcopal Zion Church: 1796-2000* by Johnson and Williams is another recent account that has provided much insight into the history of Mrs. Catherine Gillchrist Thompson of Newburgh. These recent publications along with the major historical works of the denomination remain a continual source of support.

Further mention should be made of the Roger King book, *The Silent Rebellion: The Underground Railroad in Orange County, New York*. The book gives significant credit to the members of the church for the struggle to freedom in the Underground Railroad.

In 2000, Kevin Barrett's book, *Images of America: Newburgh*, included numerous photographs related to the church and its members. Page 11 illustrates the historic Montgomery Street from a map drawn by Selah Reeve in 3806. Again, Montgomery Street remains the historic site for the local church due to its formation on this street. The local church is also proud of its distinguished members. Pages 99 through 100 mark the demolition of an old building which occupied the site where Varick Homes is now located. Pages 115, 121, 122, and 127 mark other special sites and occasions important to the local church.

ERECTED
TO THE MEMORY OF
BISHOP JOSEPH P. THOMPSON, M.D. D.D.
WHO DEVOTED HIS
LIFE'S WORK TO THE CHURCH
Died December 21, 1894.

AND TO THE MEMORY OF
MATILDA MATTHEWS
BLESSED ARE THEY THAT CONSIDER THE POOR
Died May 1, 1891.

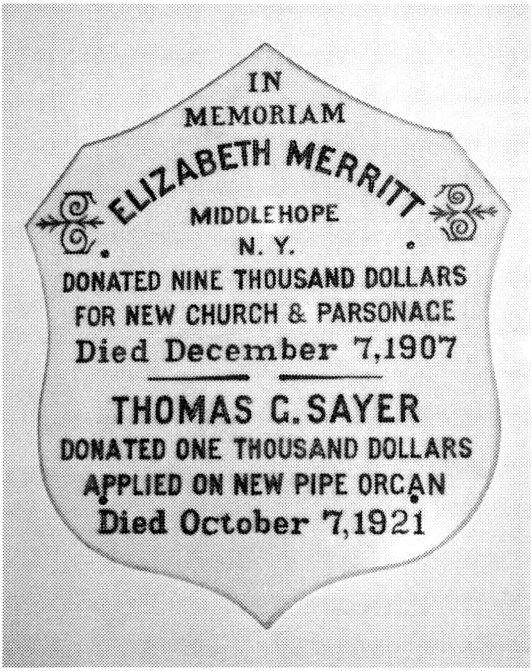

IN
MEMORIAM
ELIZABETH MERRITT
MIDDLE HOPE
N. Y.
DONATED NINE THOUSAND DOLLARS
FOR NEW CHURCH & PARSONAGE
Died December 7, 1907

THOMAS G. SAYER
DONATED ONE THOUSAND DOLLARS
APPLIED ON NEW PIPE ORGAN
Died October 7, 1921

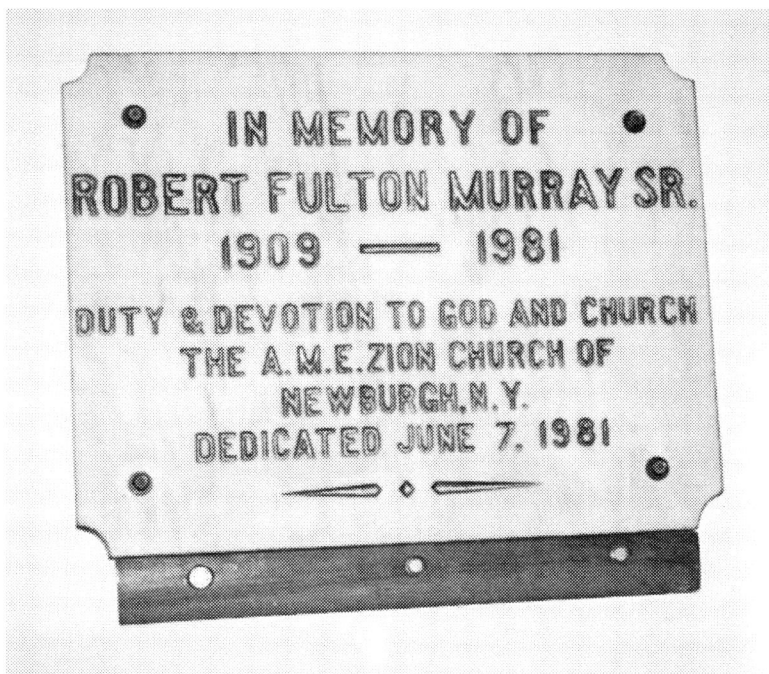

IN MEMORY OF
ROBERT FULTON MURRAY SR.
1909 — 1981
DUTY & DEVOTION TO GOD AND CHURCH
THE A.M.E. ZION CHURCH OF
NEWBURGH, N.Y.
DEDICATED JUNE 7, 1981

# CHAPTER THREE

## INDEX OF HISTORICAL CHURCH RECORDS

There are seven highly prized historical documents written by members and clerks of the African Methodist Episcopal Zion Church of Newburgh, New York. These historical documents date back to 1893 and end in the mid 1900s. All of them are handwritten documents

*The Matilda Matthews Poor Fund of the African Methodist Episcopal Zion Church of Newburgh, New York* began in 1893 and the last date recorded in the book is 1950. This is the first financial record of contributions to the local church. The first financial secretary of the fund was Mary A. Thompson Alsdorf, the daughter of Bishop and Mrs. Joseph P. Thompson. Bishop Thompson was the original trustee of the fund, appointed on July 9, 1891; he died in 1894. Then, his daughter Mary Thompson Alsdorf took charge of the fund. Then Mrs. Thompson Alsdorf died in 1914, and her son, Simon P. Alsdorf, took charge of the financial records of the fund. He took charge of the fund as its trustee until he died in 1946. Following his death, his brother Ulysses J. Alsdorf was requested to take charge of the fund. Mrs. Ulysses J. Alsdorf decided not to accept the position. In his own handwritings, he said in a letter to the Reverend J.H. Tucker, Presiding Elder and the Reverend T.C. McDougal, Pastor: "I have decided to decline the appointment in favor of a younger person." (Ulysses J. Alsdorf, May 15, 1956) The next trustee was Mr. Leonard Freeman of Newburgh, New York. The final document in the book is dated May 8, 1950.

*The Historical Record of the African Methodist Episcopal Zion Church of Newburgh, New York* is an excellent resource of local church history with a collection of articles starting in 1906 and ending with historical church records in 1950. This is a large and heavy book with pages and pages filled with articles about the church and its members. Additionally, there is a handwritten account of the history of the church beginning in 1827. Due to the many styles of handwriting, it seems as if this historical record was passed down from generation to generation beginning n the 1800s with the final person completing the book in the 1950s.

*The African Methodist Episcopal Zion Church Board of Trustees Minutes: 1905 to 1909* is a detailed account of all church activities from December 12, 1905 to June 26, 1909. Another historical account similar to this one is also preserved. *The Records of The African Methodist Episcopal Zion Church Board of Trustees: 1955 to 1964* is an account of the church with the following contributors: Venetia Bright, Milton E. Fountain, Eleanor Latham, Henrietta J. Murray, Robert Murray, and Joe L. Smith. It includes the history of the local church and minutes from 1959 to 1964.

*Membership of The African Methodist Episcopal Zion Church of Newburgh, New York from June, 1943 to August, 1944* is a financial record of the membership of the local church. The financial contributions of the members are recorded in alphabetical order from Sunday to Sunday. *The African Methodist Episcopal Zion Church Roll and Records* includes the church history from 1950 to 1957. The binding of the church roll book reads: "The African Methodist Episcopal Zion Church Sunday School, Organized November, 1849." *The Annual Dinner Book 1950 to 1961* is a social history of the church during this period. The contributing authors were Henrietta J. Murray and Robert Murray. The book begins with the third year of this traditional dinner on page 49. Pages 1-48 are missing from this book, so perhaps the previous notes from the first two dinners were located on these pages. Each chapter includes the minutes from the meetings in preparation for the dinner, a ticket, and a menu. The pastors who served the church during the Annual Dinners were T.C. McDougal, C.G. McKinney, L.C. Siler, and A. Hoggard.

Other historical documents include posters, membership lists, and historical records about the members on pieces of paper and note cards from the 1860s to the 1930s. These too are treasures highly esteemed.

# PHOTOGRAPHS

Photograph 1:   Mrs. Vivian I. Love Jones, former First Lady of the Newburgh Church and current First Lady of the New York City District, at the graves of Bishop Joseph P. Thompson, Mrs. Catherine Gilchrist Thompson, Mrs. Mary A. Thompson Alsdorf, and other heirs of the bishop of Woodlawn Cemetery, New Windsor, New York. On this day in February of 2000, the African Methodist Episcopal Zion Church of Newburgh, New York held a pilgrimage from the church to the cemetery. The church placed a wreath at the graves of Bishop and Mrs. Thompson.

Photograph 2:   The graves of the Thompson Family and other descendents.

Photograph 3:   The Frederick Douglass Monument outside the African Methodist Episcopal Zion Church of Newburgh, New York located at 111 Washington Street.

Photograph 4:   A plaque dedicated to Bishop Thompson and Mrs. Matilda Matthews on the rear wall of the sanctuary of the African Methodist Episcopal Zion Church of Newburgh, New York.

Photograph 5:   A plaque dedicated to Elizabeth Merritt and Thomas Sayer on the rear wall of the sanctuary of the African Methodist Episcopal Zion Church of Newburgh, New York.

Photograph 6:   A plaque dedicated on February 12, 1909 to the colored Volunteers of Orange County, New York who fought in the Civil War. It is on a wall in the sanctuary of the

Newburgh Church. Many of the soldiers were members of the African Methodist Episcopal Zion Church of Newburgh, New York and are buried in the "colored section" of Woodlawn Cemetery. They were honored by the local church in February of 2000 during the pilgrimage from the church to the cemetery. Church members placed red carnations on the grave of each soldier whose name was on the plaque.

Photograph 7:     A plaque dedicated to Mr. Robert Fulton Murray which hangs in the sanctuary of the local church. He was honored for being an outstanding lay person.

Photograph 8:     The Reverend Frank Edward Jones and Mrs. Vivian I. Love Jones present the "Zion Millennium Plaque" to the officers of the local church. It was the millennium gift of the pastor's family to the local church on January 1, 2000. It is a list of the pastors of the church from 1827 to 2000.

Photograph 9:     A silver offering plate held by the Reverend Frank E. Jones. It dates back to the early 1900s and was a gift to the church from the Men's Club.

Photograph 10:    A collection table that has been used in the church from generation to generation.

Photograph 11:    A photograph of Joseph P. Thompson as Pastor of the local church.

Photograph 12:    Mrs. Vivian I. Love Jones holds an historical photograph of church members from the early 1900s.

Photograph 13:    A view of the sanctuary.

Photograph 14–22: The stained glass windows of the church.

Photograph 23:    Varick Homes, named after Bishop James Varick of Newburgh, New York, a 122 unit multi-family housing development.

Photograph 24–25: The Reverend Frank E. Jones at his beloved Livingstone College and Hood Theological Seminary, Salisbury, North Carolina.

Photograph 26:    The Reverend Frank E. Jones and Mrs. Vivian I. Love Jones in the sanctuary of the African Methodist Episcopal Zion Church of Newburgh, New York.

# AUTHOR'S BIOGRAPHY

## JANET DENISE JONES

Janet was born and raised in Newburgh, New York, and was a member of the African Methodist Episcopal Zion Church of Newburgh, New York from 1971 to 2000. Her degrees are in Political Science, Communications, and Theology. She is a published author of numerous journal articles in communication and religion. She is the daughter of the Reverend Frank E. Jones and Mrs. Vivian I. Love Jones, former Pastor and First Lady of the African Methodist Episcopal Zion Church of Newburgh, New York. They are now the Presiding Elder and First Lady of the New York City District.

# CITATIONS

Barrett, Kevin. *Images of America: Newburgh*. Charleston, South Carolina: Arcadia Publishing, 2000.

Burrows, Daniel H. *Index to the Portrait and Biographical Record: Orange County, New York by the Chapman Publishing Company*. 1994.

Coutant, Daniel J. and Templeton, Anna. *Newburgh Streets: Names and Origins*. Newburgh, New York: Newburgh News, 1935.

Favata, Patricia A. Tompkins. *Newburgh, A History of the City, the Town, and New Windsor*. Newburgh, New York: Newburgh Enlarged City School District, June, 1997.

Gill, Bo. "A Church For All times" Newburgh, New York: *Times Herald Record*, 1989.

Hinkle, Ricardo. *Newburgh, NY: Portrait of a River City, Reclaiming a Waterfront Lost*. New York: City College of New York, 1998.

Johnson, Dorothy Sharpe and Williams, Lula Goolsby. *Pioneering Women of the African American Methodist Episcopal Zion Church*. Charlotte, North Caroline: A.M.E. Zion Publishing House, 1996.

Jones, Frank E. and Vivian Love Jones – Personal Interviews

King, Roger. *The Silent Rebellion: The Underground Railroad in Orange County, New York*. Monroe, New York: Library Research Associates, 1999.

Lee, Jesse. *History of Methodism in the United States of America: Beginning in 1766, and Continued Till 1809*. Baltimore, Maryland: Magill and Clime, 1810.

Pierson, George Wilson. *Tocqueville in America (Tocqueville and Beaumont in America)*. Baltimore, Maryland: The John Hopkins University Press, 1996.

Ruttenber, E.M. *History of the Town of Newburgh, 1859*. Newburgh, New York: E.M. Ruttenber & Company, January 3 1859.

Simpson, Matthew. *Cyclopedia of Methodism*. Philadelphia, P.A.: Everts & Stewart, 1878.

Tocqueville, Alexis Charles Henri Clerel de. *Democracy in America*. (De La Democratie en Amerique). Paris, France: *Gazette de France*, February, 1835.

Walls, William Jacob. *The African Methodist Episcopal Zion Church: Reality of the Black Church*. Charlotte, North Carolina: A.M.E. Zion Publishing House, 1974.

Wheeler, Benjamin Franklin. *The Varick Family*. Mobile, Alabama: 1906 (Updated Edition with New Forward by Bishop J. Clinton Hoggard, 1990).